WHO SHALL WE BE TODAY?

printed and published by
J. SALMON LTD., SEVENOAKS, ENGLAND

Printed in England ©

First I'm going to be a postman and deliver the letters.

Then I'm going to be a milkman and deliver all the milk.

This afternoon I'm going to be a teacher.

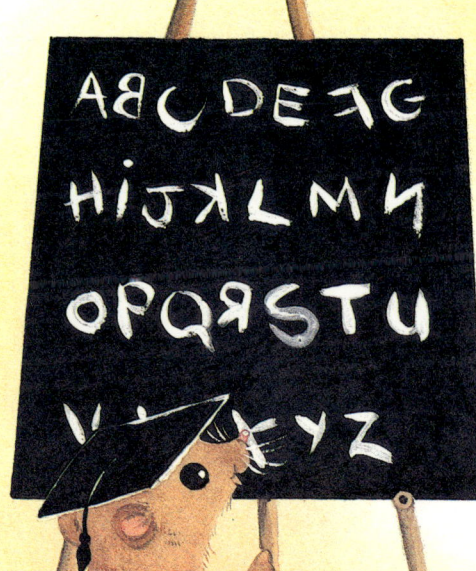

So am I.

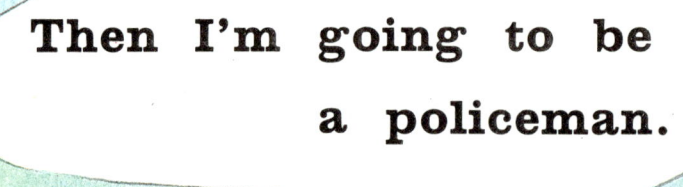

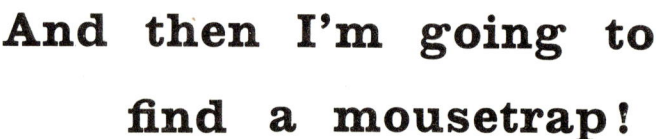